EDITORIAL

EDITORS-IN-CHIEF
Raechel Myers & Amanda Bible Williams

CONTENT DIRECTOR
Russ Ramsey, MDiv., ThM.

MANAGING EDITOR
Jessica Lamb

EDITORS
Kara Gause
Melanie Rainer

EDITORIAL ASSISTANT
Ellen Taylor

CREATIVE

CREATIVE DIRECTOR
Ryan Myers

ART DIRECTOR & DESIGNER
Kelsea Allen

ARTIST
Emily Knapp

@SHEREADSTRUTH
SHEREADSTRUTH.COM

SUBSCRIPTION INQUIRIES
orders@shereadstruth.com

SHE READS TRUTH™

© 2018 by She Reads Truth, LLC

All rights reserved.

ISBN 978-1-946282-89-7

No part of this publication may be reproduced, distributed, or transmitted in any form or by any means, including photocopying, recording, or other electronic or mechanical methods, without the prior written permission of She Reads Truth, LLC, except in the case of brief quotations embodied in critical reviews and certain other noncommercial uses permitted by copyright law.

Unless otherwise noted, all Scripture is taken from the Christian Standard Bible®. Copyright © 2017 by Holman Bible Publishers. Used by permission. Christian Standard Bible® and CSB® are federally registered trademarks of Holman Bible Publishers.

Scripture quotations marked ESV are from ESV® Bible (The Holy Bible, English Standard Version®), copyright © 2001 by Crossway, a publishing ministry of Good News Publishers. Used by permission. All rights reserved.

Though the Greek and Hebrew referenced in this book have been carefully researched, scholars disagree on how to interpret the original texts.

This book was printed offset in Nashville, Tennessee, on 70# Lynx Opaque. Cover is 100# Cougar Opaque with a soft touch lamination.

NAMES OF GOD

SHE READS TRUTH

EDITOR'S LETTER

> Our God defies simple explanation.

My given name is Amanda Jane. Our family name was Bible, and I went through school drawing a lowercase "ajb" on everything from notebooks to yearbooks to CD cases.

My grandmother called me "Doozie," which I always loved, and my brother, who insists on nicknaming everyone he knows, still calls me "Manners" (pronounced MAH-ners). My friends have also assigned me names over the years. I've been Jane, AJ, A-dubs, and yes, even Bible. A few college girlfriends call me "Scramanda" to this day, though I can't for the life of me remember why. It makes me smile anyway.

When our team set out to create a Scripture reading plan focused on the names of God, I expected it to be almost as simple. In the same way I can list the greatest hits of names I've been given throughout my life, I assumed we would list the names of God most commonly used in Scripture and offer a simple explanation of each.

But our God defies simple explanation. The deeper our editorial team dug into the text, the more complex the topic became.

God goes by many names in the Bible. Some names are mentioned only once; others appear on nearly every page. All reveal nuanced and important aspects of God's character. Some names of God are given in Hebrew while others are in Aramaic or Greek. (See the chart on page 14 to learn about the languages used in the Bible.) Some names are common words elevated to divine purposes—like Lord, which essentially means "sir." Other names are descriptive words meant to show how uncommon God is—like living God, which sets Him apart from idols of wood and stone. Some names we thought would abound in the pages of Scripture, like Jehovah, are nowhere to be found, except for a few mentions in some early English translations. (Don't miss the infographic on page 20 about the origin of the word "Jehovah." It's fascinating!)

In the end, this reading plan surprised each one of us who had a hand in putting it together. As we spent time in the pages of Scripture learning about the names of God, we were moved to worship. We were moved to tears. We became frustrated and delighted and exasperated as our finite minds tried to define the infinite God in all His fullness. And while we are certain the book you hold in your hands falls short of the perfection of the Holy One, we pray He will use it to welcome you into His Word and give you a glimpse of His goodness, majesty, power, and grace.

For the glory and honor of His great name,

Amanda

Amanda Bible Williams
EDITOR-IN-CHIEF

DESIGN ON PURPOSE

> Each unique piece is a visual reminder that each name describes an aspect of the same God.

We had an emotional response to reading about the names included in this plan, an amplified sense of the quiet reverence and awe we've felt when viewing a work of art in a gallery or museum. Our design for *Names of God* was inspired by this gallery feeling.

Our in-house artist, Emily, created unique pieces of art using strips of balsa wood on waxy palette paper. The continuity of color and texture between each unique piece is a visual reminder that each name describes an aspect of the same God. We also used this technique for the drop caps scattered throughout.

The dark jewel tones you'll see in this book are meant to further emphasize the majesty of God. We flooded the pages with a cool gray to contrast the white pages we typically use in our study books.

We chose to feature a font with great small capitals, Mrs Eaves, in the daily reading because of the significance of "Lord" in our English translations of the Bible (read more about this on page 16). Myriad Pro, which offers English, Greek, and Hebrew characters, is simple and uncomplicated, making it a fitting counterpart to the expressive Mrs Eaves.

We hope the design choices in this book serve you well as you study these names of God.

THE SHE READS TRUTH CREATIVE TEAM

HOW TO USE THIS BOOK

She Reads Truth is a community of women dedicated to reading the Word of God every day.

The Bible is living and active, breathed out by God, and we confidently hold it higher than anything we can do or say. This book focuses primarily on Scripture, with bonus resources to facilitate deeper engagement with God's Word.

SCRIPTURE READING

Designed for a Monday start, this study book presents over fifteen names of God through daily Scripture readings.

The English translation of the day's name is marked in bold when it appears as a name in the Scripture reading. The first occurrence of each distinct name is noted in the margins.

JOURNALING SPACE

Each daily reading includes a journaling prompt with space to respond.

GRACE DAY

Use Saturdays to pray, rest, and reflect on what you've read.

For added community and conversation, join us in the **Names of God** reading plan on the She Reads Truth app or at SheReadsTruth.com.

WEEKLY TRUTH

Sundays are set aside for weekly Scripture memorization.

Find the corresponding memory cards in the back of this book.

HOW TO USE THE DAILY INTRODUCTIONS

FATHER

NAME
The name featured in the daily reading.

אָב — πατήρ

AB (Hebrew) — PATER (Greek)

TRANSLITERATION
The name presented in its English pronunciation.

The personal, familial, and intimate name for God

KEY OCCURRENCES
DT 32:6; PS 68:5; JR 3:19; MT 6:9; MK 14:36; LK 11:2; RM 8:15; GL 4:6

When Jesus taught His disciples to pray, He told them to address God as "our Father" (Mt 6:9). When He prayed in the Garden of Gethsemane before His arrest, trial, and crucifixion, Jesus cried out, "*Abba*, Father," using personal and relational names for God (Mk 14:36). *Abba* is an Aramaic word, from the Hebrew *Ab*, for "father." *Pater* is the Greek word used for "father."

These are deeply familial names when used to address God. Belief brings us into a close yet respectful relationship with God, the holy Creator of all things. Father is a reverential yet personal name for God.

DESCRIPTION
An explanation of how the name is used throughout Scripture.

EMPHASIS
A short summary of the characteristic of God emphasized by the name.

KEY OCCURENCES
References to specific key verses where the name appears in Scripture.

SHE READS TRUTH

TABLE OF CONTENTS

WEEK

1

DAY 1	16
YAHWEH	
DAY 2	23
GOD	
DAY 3	26
LORD	
DAY 4	31
GOD WITH US	
DAY 5	35
HOLY ONE	
DAY 6	39
GRACE DAY	
DAY 7	40
WEEKLY TRUTH	

EXTRAS

14 *The Languages of the Bible*

20 *Where Do We Get the Word "Jehovah"?*

62 *Why Does the Bible Describe God in Physical Terms?*

72 *What Does Scripture Say About God's Name?*

96 *For the Record*

WEEK

2

DAY 8	42
LORD OF ARMIES	

DAY 9	46
SPIRIT	

DAY 10	51
LIVING GOD & GOD MOST HIGH	

DAY 11	55
GOD ALMIGHTY	

DAY 12	59
REFUGE & FORTRESS	

DAY 13	65
GRACE DAY	

DAY 14	66
WEEKLY TRUTH	

WEEK

3

DAY 15	68
JEALOUS GOD	

DAY 16	74
SHEPHERD	

DAY 17	79
FATHER	

DAY 18	82
MESSIAH	

DAY 19	87
JESUS	

DAY 20	91
GRACE DAY	

DAY 21	92
WEEKLY TRUTH	

KEY VERSE

"I am the Lord. That is my name,
and I will not give my glory to another
or my praise to idols."

ISAIAH 42:8

THE LANGUAGES OF THE BIBLE

God gave us the Bible so we can know Him and His story. He used people who spoke in ancient Hebrew, Aramaic, and Greek to write the books of the Bible. We can learn more about our unchanging God by seeing how He revealed Himself and His Word in these original contexts.

HEBREW

The thirty-nine books of the Old Testament were written over a 1,500-year period in mostly classical Hebrew. This was the language of Moses, David, and the Israelite people.

The Hebrew language is read from right to left and originally had no written vowels or punctuation. Some Hebrew words, like *amen* and *hosanna*, are written phonetically in Greek in the New Testament.

ARAMAIC

When the Israelite people lived in exile, the Hebrew language was almost completely replaced in everyday conversation by ancient Aramaic. While Hebrew remained the primary written language of Scripture, a few passages in the Old Testament from this period were written in Aramaic (Jr 10:11; Dn 2:4b–7:28; Ezr 4:8–6:18; 7:12–26). The name of a location in Genesis 31:47 is also given in both Aramaic and Hebrew. Aramaic and Hebrew are similar enough that a reader of one can often read some of the other.

Aramaic remained the most common language in Israel into the first century AD. Aramaic words and names written phonetically in Greek are scattered throughout the New Testament (e.g., Mk 5:41; 7:34; Mt 27:46).

GREEK

During the second and third centuries BC, the Old Testament was translated into Greek, the most prevalent language of the region. This translation, later called the Septuagint, was widely read in synagogues during the intertestamental period and the first century AD.

By the time the New Testament was written, Israel was part of the Roman Empire. The ability to speak in multiple languages and understand basic Greek was widespread across the entire region. When the authors of the New Testament wrote their texts, they wrote in the popular language of Koine Greek. This was the common, everyday Greek spoken by people across the Empire regardless of income, education, or social status.

OLD TESTAMENT

The Old Testament was written primarily in Hebrew, with a few passages in Aramaic.

NEW TESTAMENT

The New Testament was written in Greek. It contains a few Aramaic words and phrases, Hebrew words, and Hebrew and Aramaic names, but all are written in Greek letters.

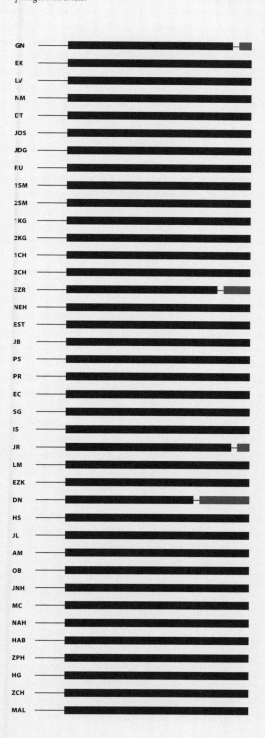

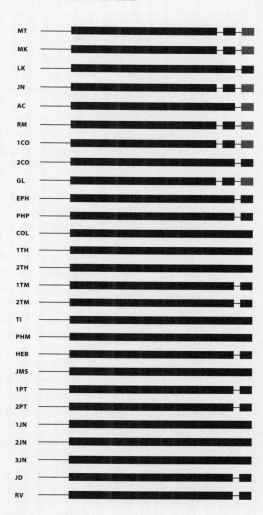

SHE READS TRUTH 15

YAHWEH

יהוה

YHWH

Hebrew

The name God gives Himself, highlighting His covenantal and relational nature

KEY OCCURRENCES
EX 3:15; 34:6; DT 1:10;
PS 15:1; IS 42:8

Yahweh is a profoundly holy name, but it is also unmistakably personal. *Yahweh* is distinct from other names of God because it is self-revealed. It is the intimate, covenantal, relational name of God. Modern English translations of the Bible often use small capital letters (LORD or GOD) for *YHWH*.

When Moses asks God for His name in Exodus 3, God reveals Himself as "I Am Who I Am," and then calls Himself *Yahweh*. In Exodus 34, He again proclaims His name as He describes His character to Moses. His name is a core part of the covenantal promise He makes with Moses—*Yahweh* will always be who He is.

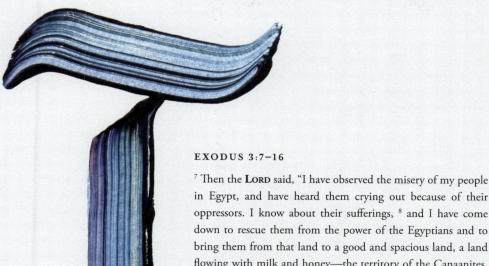

EXODUS 3:7–16

⁷ Then the LORD said, "I have observed the misery of my people in Egypt, and have heard them crying out because of their oppressors. I know about their sufferings, ⁸ and I have come down to rescue them from the power of the Egyptians and to bring them from that land to a good and spacious land, a land flowing with milk and honey—the territory of the Canaanites, Hethites, Amorites, Perizzites, Hivites, and Jebusites. ⁹ So because the Israelites' cry for help has come to me, and I have also seen the way the Egyptians are oppressing them, ¹⁰ therefore, go. I am sending you to Pharaoh so that you may lead my people, the Israelites, out of Egypt."

¹¹ But Moses asked God, "Who am I that I should go to Pharaoh and that I should bring the Israelites out of Egypt?"

¹² He answered, "I will certainly be with you, and this will be the sign to you that I am the one who sent you: when you bring the people out of Egypt, you will all worship God at this mountain."

¹³ Then Moses asked God, "If I go to the Israelites and say to them, 'The God of your fathers has sent me to you,' and they ask me, 'What is his name?' what should I tell them?"

¹⁴ God replied to Moses, "I AM WHO I AM. This is what you are to say to the Israelites: I AM has sent me to you." ¹⁵ God also said to Moses, "Say this to the Israelites: The LORD, the God of your fathers, the God of Abraham, the God of Isaac, and the God of Jacob, has sent me to you. This is my name forever; this is how I am to be remembered in every generation.

¹⁶ "Go and assemble the elders of Israel and say to them: The LORD, the God of your fathers, the God of Abraham, Isaac,

YAHWEH
Lord - English translation of Yahweh

and Jacob, has appeared to me and said: I have paid close attention to you and to what has been done to you in Egypt."

EXODUS 34:1–9

New Stone Tablets

¹ The LORD said to Moses, "Cut two stone tablets like the first ones, and I will write on them the words that were on the first tablets, which you broke. ² Be prepared by morning. Come up Mount Sinai in the morning and stand before me on the mountaintop. ³ No one may go up with you; in fact, no one should be seen anywhere on the mountain. Even the flocks and herds are not to graze in front of that mountain."

⁴ Moses cut two stone tablets like the first ones. He got up early in the morning, and taking the two stone tablets in his hand, he climbed Mount Sinai, just as the LORD had commanded him.

⁵ The LORD came down in a cloud, stood with him there, and proclaimed his name, "the LORD." ⁶ The LORD passed in front of him and proclaimed:

The LORD—the LORD is a compassionate and gracious God, slow to anger and abounding in faithful love and truth, ⁷ maintaining faithful love to a thousand generations, forgiving iniquity, rebellion, and sin. But he will not leave the guilty unpunished, bringing the fathers' iniquity on the children and grandchildren to the third and fourth generation.

⁸ Moses immediately knelt low on the ground and worshiped. ⁹ Then he said, "My Lord, if I have indeed found favor with you, my Lord, please go with us (even though this is a stiff-necked people), forgive our iniquity and our sin, and accept us as your own possession."

PSALM 15

A Description of the Godly
A psalm of David.

¹ LORD, who can dwell in your tent?
Who can live on your holy mountain?

² The one who lives blamelessly, practices righteousness,
and acknowledges the truth in his heart—
³ who does not slander with his tongue,
who does not harm his friend
or discredit his neighbor,
⁴ who despises the one rejected by the LORD
but honors those who fear the LORD,
who keeps his word whatever the cost,
⁵ who does not lend his silver at interest
or take a bribe against the innocent—
the one who does these things will never be shaken.

ISAIAH 42:5–9

⁵ This is what God, the LORD, says—
who created the heavens and stretched them out,
who spread out the earth and what comes from it,
who gives breath to the people on it
and spirit to those who walk on it—
⁶ "I am the LORD. I have called you
for a righteous purpose,
and I will hold you by your hand.
I will watch over you, and I will appoint you
to be a covenant for the people
and a light to the nations,
⁷ in order to open blind eyes,
to bring out prisoners from the dungeon,
and those sitting in darkness from the prison house.
⁸ I am the LORD. That is my name,
and I will not give my glory to another
or my praise to idols.
⁹ The past events have indeed happened.
Now I declare new events;
I announce them to you before they occur."

JOHN 8:58

Jesus said to them, "Truly I tell you, before Abraham was, I am."

YAHWEH

What does this name
teach me about God?

Each name describes specific character of God

WHERE DO WE GET THE WORD "JEHOVAH"?

The word "Jehovah" never appears in the original Hebrew. So where did it come from?

The personal name of God, *YHWH* (*Yahweh*), stopped being spoken aloud by the Hebrew people sometime in the third century BC. Instead, when they came to this written name in the Old Testament, they would say the Hebrew word for "lord," *adonay*. Modern English translations of the Bible often use small capital letters (Lord or God) for *YHWH*. (See Day 1.)

In the sixth century AD, a group of Jewish scholars and scribes added vowels to the Hebrew consonants. When they reached *YHWH*, they added the vowels from *adonay* below the word as a reminder to not speak the personal name of God. Some early English translations introduced the word "Jehovah" as a combination of what was written and what was meant to be spoken by combining the vowels from *adonay* with the consonants of *YHWH*.

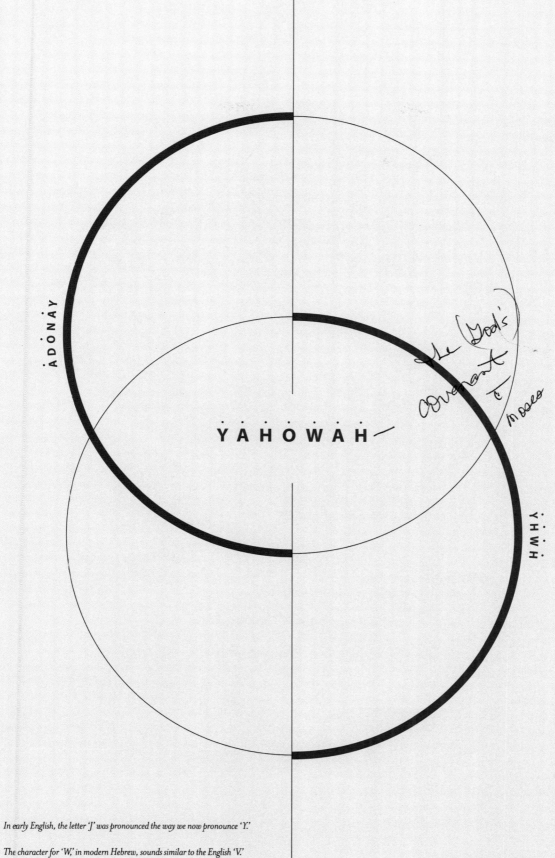

ADONAY

YAHOWAH

YHWH

In early English, the letter 'J' was pronounced the way we now pronounce 'Y.'

The character for 'W,' in modern Hebrew, sounds similar to the English 'V.'

GOD

אֵל

EL

Hebrew

אֱלֹהִים

ELOHIM

Hebrew

God's unmatched power and majesty

KEY OCCURRENCES
GN 1:1; JB 37:5; PS 42:2; IS 43:12; JNH 1:9

Elohim is the first name used for God in the Bible. It appears in the opening verse of Scripture: "In the beginning God created the heavens and the earth" (Gn 1:1). The Israelites adapted the name *Elohim* from *El*, an ancient word for "god," to refer to the one true God. This name emphasizes His greatness and majesty over all creation and all other gods. Throughout Scripture this name is paired with descriptive words to distinguish God and His character from pagan gods (e.g., *El Olam*, "everlasting God," *El Roi*, "God who sees," and *El Rahum*, "merciful God"). *Elohim* is a reminder that the one true God is distinctly powerful.

GENESIS 1:1–5

The Creation

ELOHIM

¹ In the beginning **God** created the heavens and the earth.

² Now the earth was formless and empty, darkness covered the surface of the watery depths, and the Spirit of **God** was hovering over the surface of the waters. ³ Then **God** said, "Let there be light," and there was light. ⁴ **God** saw that the light was good, and **God** separated the light from the darkness. ⁵ **God** called the light "day," and the darkness he called "night." There was an evening, and there was a morning: one day.

JOB 37:5–13

EL

⁵ **God** thunders wondrously with
   his voice;
he does great things that we cannot
   comprehend.

⁶ For he says to the snow, "Fall to the earth,"
and the torrential rains, his mighty torrential rains,
⁷ serve as his sign to all mankind,
so that all men may know his work.
⁸ The wild animals enter their lairs
and stay in their dens.
⁹ The windstorm comes from its chamber,
and the cold from the driving north winds.
¹⁰ Ice is formed by the breath of **God**,
and watery expanses are frozen.
¹¹ He saturates clouds with moisture;
he scatters his lightning through them.
¹² They swirl about,
turning round and round at his direction,
accomplishing everything he commands them
over the surface of the inhabited world.
¹³ He causes this to happen for punishment,
for his land, or for his faithful love.

PSALM 42:1–11 ESV

Why Are You Cast Down, O My Soul?
To the choirmaster. A Maskil of the Sons of Korah.

¹ As a deer pants for flowing streams,
so pants my soul for you, O **God**.
² My soul thirsts for **God**,
for the living **God**.
When shall I come and appear before **God**?
³ My tears have been my food
day and night,
while they say to me all the day long,
"Where is your **God**?"
⁴ These things I remember,
as I pour out my soul:
how I would go with the throng
and lead them in procession to the house of **God**
with glad shouts and songs of praise,
a multitude keeping festival.

⁵ Why are you cast down, O my soul,
and why are you in turmoil within me?
Hope in **God**; for I shall again praise him,
my salvation ⁶ and my **God**.

My soul is cast down within me;
therefore I remember you
from the land of Jordan and of Hermon,
from Mount Mizar.
⁷ Deep calls to deep
at the roar of your waterfalls;
all your breakers and your waves
have gone over me.
⁸ By day the Lᴏʀᴅ commands his steadfast love,
and at night his song is with me,
a prayer to the **God** of my life.
⁹ I say to **God**, my rock:
"Why have you forgotten me?
Why do I go mourning
because of the oppression of the enemy?"

¹⁰ As with a deadly wound in my bones,
my adversaries taunt me,
while they say to me all the day long,
"Where is your **God**?"

¹¹ Why are you cast down, O my soul,
and why are you in turmoil within me?
Hope in **God**; for I shall again praise him,
my salvation and my **God**.

ISAIAH 43:10–13 ESV

¹⁰ "You are my witnesses," declares the Lord,
"and my servant whom I have chosen,
that you may know and believe me
and understand that I am he.
Before me no god was formed,
nor shall there be any after me.
¹¹ I, I am the Lord,
and besides me there is no savior.
¹² I declared and saved and proclaimed,
when there was no strange god among you;
and you are my witnesses," declares the Lord,
    "and I am **God**.
¹³ Also henceforth I am he;
there is none who can deliver from my hand;
I work, and who can turn it back?"

GOD

What does this name teach me about God?

LORD

אֲדֹנָי	κύριος
ADONAY	KURIOS
Hebrew	*Greek*

A title of honor, respecting the authority and ruling power of God

KEY OCCURRENCES
EX 15:17; DT 10:17; MT 14:28; JN 20:25; RM 8:39; 1CO 8:6; EPH 6:10; RV 17:14

In the Old Testament, *adonay*, or "lord," was a common way to refer to God. It comes from the word used to describe human masters who ruled over servants. The Israelites used it verbally instead of pronouncing the name *Yahweh*, and it communicated their reverence for the Holy God of Israel as their ruler and ultimate authority. *Adonay* is a reminder that we serve a holy, sovereign God who is Lord over all.

Kurios, or "lord" in the New Testament, was used to show respect to people with authority, like emperors or masters. It is used to describe both God the Father and Jesus the Son in the New Testament. When followers of Jesus called Him "lord," they showed Him honor. In Paul's letters, he used the word as a title for the risen Jesus. "Lord Jesus Christ" became a primary way to refer to Him, implying He shared the authority of the God of Israel. *Kurios* is a powerful name of honor for Jesus.

GENESIS 15:1–6

The Abrahamic Covenant

¹ After these events, the word of the Lord came to Abram in a vision:

> Do not be afraid, Abram.
> I am your shield;
> your reward will be very great.

² But Abram said, "**Lord** God, what can you give me, since I am childless and the heir of my house is Eliezer of Damascus?" ³ Abram continued, "Look, you have given me no offspring, so a slave born in my house will be my heir."

——————— ADONAY

⁴ Now the word of the Lord came to him: "This one will not be your heir; instead, one who comes from your own body will be your heir." ⁵ He took him outside and said, "Look at the sky and count the stars, if you are able to count them." Then he said to him, "Your offspring will be that numerous."

⁶ Abram believed the Lord, and he credited it to him as righteousness.

EXODUS 4:10–16

¹⁰ But Moses replied to the Lord, "Please, **Lord**, I have never been eloquent—either in the past or recently or since you have been speaking to your servant—because my mouth and my tongue are sluggish."

¹¹ The LORD said to him, "Who placed a mouth on humans? Who makes a person mute or deaf, seeing or blind? Is it not I, the LORD? ¹² Now go! I will help you speak and I will teach you what to say."

¹³ Moses said, "Please, **Lord**, send someone else."

¹⁴ Then the LORD's anger burned against Moses, and he said, "Isn't Aaron the Levite your brother? I know that he can speak well. And also, he is on his way now to meet you. He will rejoice when he sees you. ¹⁵ You will speak with him and tell him what to say. I will help both you and him to speak and will teach you both what to do. ¹⁶ He will speak to the people for you. He will serve as a mouth for you, and you will serve as God to him."

DEUTERONOMY 10:17–21

¹⁷ For the LORD your God is the God of gods and **Lord** of lords, the great, mighty, and awe-inspiring God, showing no partiality and taking no bribe. ¹⁸ He executes justice for the fatherless and the widow, and loves the resident alien, giving him food and clothing. ¹⁹ You are also to love the resident alien, since you were resident aliens in the land of Egypt. ²⁰ You are to fear the LORD your God and worship him. Remain faithful to him and take oaths in his name. ²¹ He is your praise and he is your God, who has done for you these great and awe-inspiring works your eyes have seen.

MATTHEW 14:22–32

Walking on the Water

²² Immediately he made the disciples get into the boat and go ahead of him to the other side, while he dismissed the crowds. ²³ After dismissing the crowds, he went up on the mountain by himself to pray. Well into the night, he was there alone. ²⁴ Meanwhile, the boat was already some distance from land, battered by the waves, because the wind was against them. ²⁵ Jesus came toward them walking on the sea very early in the morning. ²⁶ When the disciples saw him walking on the sea, they were terrified. "It's a ghost!" they said, and they cried out in fear.

²⁷ Immediately Jesus spoke to them. "Have courage! It is I. Don't be afraid."

²⁸ "**Lord**, if it's you," Peter answered him, "command me to come to you on the water."

KURIOS

²⁹ He said, "Come."

And climbing out of the boat, Peter started walking on the water and came toward Jesus. ³⁰ But when he saw the strength of the wind, he was afraid, and beginning to sink he cried out, "**Lord**, save me!"

³¹ Immediately Jesus reached out his hand, caught hold of him, and said to him, "You of little faith, why did you doubt?"

³² When they got into the boat, the wind ceased.

JOHN 20:24–29

Thomas Sees and Believes

²⁴ But Thomas (called "Twin"), one of the Twelve, was not with them when Jesus came. ²⁵ So the other disciples were telling him, "We've seen the **Lord**!"

But he said to them, "If I don't see the mark of the nails in his hands, put my finger into the mark of the nails, and put my hand into his side, I will never believe."

²⁶ A week later his disciples were indoors again, and Thomas was with them. Even though the doors were locked, Jesus came and stood among them and said, "Peace be with you."

²⁷ Then he said to Thomas, "Put your finger here and look at my hands. Reach out your hand and put it into my side. Don't be faithless, but believe."

²⁸ Thomas responded to him, "My **Lord** and my God!"

²⁹ Jesus said, "Because you have seen me, you have believed. Blessed are those who have not seen and yet believe."

1 CORINTHIANS 8:5–6

⁵ For even if there are so-called gods, whether in heaven or on earth—as there are many "gods" and many "lords"— ⁶ yet for us there is one God, the Father. All things are from him, and we exist for him. And there is one **Lord**, Jesus Christ. All things are through him, and we exist through him.

REVELATION 17:14

These will make war against the Lamb, but the Lamb will conquer them because he is **Lord** of lords and King of kings. Those with him are called, chosen, and faithful.

LORD

What does this name teach me about God?

4

GOD WITH US

עִמָּנוּאֵל

IMMANUEL

Hebrew

Ἐμμανουήλ

IMMANUEL

Greek

God's nearness to and presence with His people

KEY OCCURRENCES
IS 7:14; 8:8; MT 1:23

The name *Immanuel*, or "God is with us," appears in the book of Isaiah in key prophecies predicting the coming of the Messiah. The name carries a sense of nearness, including intimate knowledge of the needs, struggles, and hopes of humanity. When Isaiah prophesies about the virgin birth, he says that her child will be called *Immanuel*. This is not a proper name as much as it is a description of what the Messiah would be like.

In Matthew, an angel tells Joseph to name the child Jesus, because "He will save His people from their sins" (Mt 1:21). This name describes what *Immanuel* would do. Together, the names *Immanuel* and Jesus mean "God will be with His people and He will save them from their sins." God saves His people and is close to them.

IMMANUEL

ISAIAH 7:13–17

[13] Isaiah said, "Listen, house of David! Is it not enough for you to try the patience of men? Will you also try the patience of my God? [14] Therefore, the Lord himself will give you a sign:

See, the virgin will conceive, have a son, and name him **Immanuel**.

[15] By the time he learns to reject what is bad and choose what is good, he will be eating curds and honey. [16] For before the boy knows to reject what is bad and choose what is good, the land of the two kings you dread will be abandoned. [17] The LORD will bring on you, your people, and your father's house such a time as has never been since Ephraim separated from Judah: He will bring the king of Assyria."

MATTHEW 1:18–25

The Nativity of the Christ

[18] The birth of Jesus Christ came about this way: After his mother Mary had been engaged to Joseph, it was discovered before they came together that she was pregnant from the Holy Spirit. [19] So her husband Joseph, being a righteous man, and not wanting to disgrace her publicly, decided to divorce her secretly.

[20] But after he had considered these things, an angel of the Lord appeared to him in a dream, saying, "Joseph, son of David, don't be afraid to take Mary as your wife, because what has been conceived in her is from the Holy Spirit. [21] She will give birth to a son, and you are to name him Jesus, because he will save his people from their sins."

[22] Now all this took place to fulfill what was spoken by the Lord through the prophet:

[23] See, the virgin will become pregnant
and give birth to a son,
and they will name him **Immanuel**,

which is translated "God is with us."

[24] When Joseph woke up, he did as the Lord's angel had commanded him. He married her [25] but did not have sexual relations with her until she gave birth to a son. And he named him Jesus.

MATTHEW 28:19–20

[19] "Go, therefore, and make disciples of all nations, baptizing them in the name of the Father and of the Son and of the Holy Spirit, [20] teaching them to observe everything I have commanded you. And remember, I am with you always, to the end of the age."

JOHN 1:10–18

[10] He was in the world, and the world was created through him, and yet the world did not recognize him. [11] He came to his own, and his own people did not receive him. [12] But to all who did receive him, he gave them the right to be children of God, to those who believe in his name, [13] who were born, not of natural descent, or of the will of the flesh, or of the will of man, but of God.

[14] The Word became flesh and dwelt among us. We observed his glory, the glory as the one and only Son from the Father, full of grace and truth. [15] (John testified concerning him and exclaimed, "This was the one of whom I said, 'The one coming after me ranks ahead of me, because he existed before me.'") [16] Indeed, we have all received grace upon grace from his fullness, [17] for the law was given through Moses; grace and truth came through Jesus Christ. [18] No one has ever seen God. The one and only Son, who is himself God and is at the Father's side—he has revealed him.

REVELATION 21:3

Then I heard a loud voice from the throne: Look, God's dwelling is with humanity, and he will live with them. They will be his peoples, and God himself will be with them and will be their God.

GOD WITH US

What does this name
teach me about God?

HOLY ONE

קָדוֹשׁ

QADOSH

Hebrew

The righteousness and holiness of God

KEY OCCURRENCES
2KG 19:22; JB 6:10; PS 78:41; 89:18; IS 41:14; 54:5

The Hebrew word *qadosh* is translated "set apart as holy." It can be used in a general sense to describe places, objects, and people who have been set apart for religious purposes. But as a name, *Qadosh*, or "Holy One," describes God as one who is set apart from His creation, from all pagan gods, and from everything else because of His perfection. This name works like a double-edged sword: it reminds us that God is perfectly holy in every way, and it reminds us that we are not. The distinction of being the Holy One belongs to Him alone. This name exalts God above all others in His holiness.

QADOSH

PSALM 78:40–43

⁴⁰ How often they rebelled against him
in the wilderness
and grieved him in the desert.
⁴¹ They constantly tested God
and provoked the **Holy One** of Israel.
⁴² They did not remember his power shown
on the day he redeemed them from the foe,
⁴³ when he performed his miraculous signs in Egypt
and his wonders in the territory of Zoan.

PSALM 89:15–18

¹⁵ Happy are the people who know the joyful shout;
Lord, they walk in the light from your face.
¹⁶ They rejoice in your name all day long,
and they are exalted by your righteousness.
¹⁷ For you are their magnificent strength;
by your favor our horn is exalted.
¹⁸ Surely our shield belongs to the Lord,
our king to the **Holy One** of Israel.

ISAIAH 41:12–20

¹² You will look for those who contend with you,
but you will not find them.
Those who war against you
will become absolutely nothing.
¹³ For I am the Lord your God,
who holds your right hand,
who says to you, 'Do not fear,
I will help you.
¹⁴ Do not fear, you worm Jacob,
you men of Israel.
I will help you'—
 this is the Lord's declaration.
Your Redeemer is the **Holy One** of Israel.
¹⁵ See, I will make you into a sharp threshing board,
new, with many teeth.
You will thresh mountains and pulverize them
and make hills into chaff.
¹⁶ You will winnow them
and a wind will carry them away,
a whirlwind will scatter them.

But you will rejoice in the Lord;
you will boast in the **Holy One** of Israel.

¹⁷ The poor and the needy seek water, but there is none;
their tongues are parched with thirst.
I will answer them.
I am the Lord, the God of Israel. I will not
abandon them.
¹⁸ I will open rivers on the barren heights,
and springs in the middle of the plains.
I will turn the desert into a pool
and dry land into springs.
¹⁹ I will plant cedars,
acacias, myrtles, and olive trees in the wilderness.
I will put juniper trees,
elms, and cypress trees together in the desert,
²⁰ so that all may see and know,
consider and understand,
that the hand of the Lord has done this,
the **Holy One** of Israel has created it.

REVELATION 4:1–8

The Throne Room of Heaven

¹ After this I looked, and there in heaven was an open door. The first voice that I had heard speaking to me like a trumpet said, "Come up here, and I will show you what must take place after this."

² Immediately I was in the Spirit, and there was a throne in heaven and someone was seated on it. ³ The one seated there had the appearance of jasper and carnelian stone. A rainbow that had the appearance of an emerald surrounded the throne.

⁴ Around the throne were twenty-four thrones, and on the thrones sat twenty-four elders dressed in white clothes, with golden crowns on their heads.

⁵ Flashes of lightning and rumblings and peals of thunder came from the throne. Seven fiery torches were burning before the throne, which are the seven spirits of God. ⁶ Something like a sea of glass, similar to crystal, was also before the throne.

Four living creatures covered with eyes in front and in back were around the throne on each side. ⁷ The first living creature was like a lion; the second living creature was like an ox; the third living creature had a face like a man; and the fourth living creature was like a flying eagle. ⁸ Each of the four living creatures had six wings; they were covered with eyes around and inside. Day and night they never stop, saying,

> Holy, holy, holy,
> Lord God, the Almighty,
> who was, who is, and who is to come.

HOLY ONE

What does this name teach me about God?

GRACE DAY

χάρις

CHARIS

Grace

Use this day to pray, rest, and reflect on this week's reading, giving thanks for the grace that is ours in Christ.

For even if there are so-called gods, whether in heaven or on earth—as there are many "gods" and many "lords"— yet for us there is one God, the Father. All things are from him, and we exist for him. And there is one Lord, Jesus Christ. All things are through him, and we exist through him.

1 CORINTHIANS 8:5–6

7

WEEKLY TRUTH

ἀλήθεια

ALÊTHEIA

Truth

Scripture is God-breathed and true. When we memorize it, we carry the gospel with us wherever we go.

This week we will memorize the key verse for this reading plan, which powerfully summarizes the supremacy of God's name.

"I am the LORD. That is my name,
and I will not give my glory to another
or my praise to idols."

ISAIAH 42:8

Find the corresponding memory card in the back of this book.

LORD OF ARMIES

אֱלֹהִים צְבָאוֹת	יהוה אֱלֹהִים צְבָאוֹת	יהוה צְבָאוֹת
ELOHIM TSEBAOTH	YAHWEH ELOHIM TSEBACTH	YAHWEH TSEBAOTH
Hebrew	*Hebrew*	*Hebrew*

The security, power, and strength of God in the face of His enemies

KEY OCCURRENCES

1SM 1:11; 2SM 7:26; PS 80:7; IS 9:7; AM 5:14–15; HG 2:6; MAL 1:11; 2:2

The Hebrew root word *tsaba*, or "a gathering of people," is frequently used in the Bible to describe armies preparing for war. When paired with the name of God in *Yahweh Tsebaoth*, it reveres Him as being over hosts of angelic armies who gather in His name and serve at His command. All creation is subject to the Lord of Armies. "Lord of Hosts," "God of Armies," and "Lord God of Armies" are versions of this name.

"Lord of Armies" most frequently appears in the Minor Prophets, especially in Malachi, where almost half of the verses in the book contain this name in some form. During the time of the prophets, the people of God were living in exile in Babylon. They faced daily reminders of the presence and power of the enemy armies that kept them in captivity. They called out to God as the Lord of Armies, whose vast angelic hosts could deliver them from trouble. Lord of Armies is a name that assures us of the power of our mighty God.

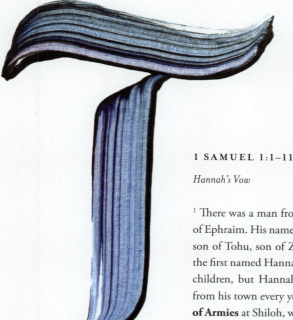

1 SAMUEL 1:1–11

Hannah's Vow

¹ There was a man from Ramathaim-zophim in the hill country of Ephraim. His name was Elkanah son of Jeroham, son of Elihu, son of Tohu, son of Zuph, an Ephraimite. ² He had two wives, the first named Hannah and the second Peninnah. Peninnah had children, but Hannah was childless. ³ This man would go up from his town every year to worship and to sacrifice to the **Lord of Armies** at Shiloh, where Eli's two sons, Hophni and Phinehas, were the Lord's priests.

YAHWEH TSEBAOTH

⁴ Whenever Elkanah offered a sacrifice, he always gave portions of the meat to his wife Peninnah and to each of her sons and daughters. ⁵ But he gave a double portion to Hannah, for he loved her even though the Lord had kept her from conceiving. ⁶ Her rival would taunt her severely just to provoke her, because the Lord had kept Hannah from conceiving. ⁷ Year after year, when she went up to the Lord's house, her rival taunted her in this way. Hannah would weep and would not eat. ⁸ "Hannah, why are you crying?" her husband Elkanah would ask. "Why won't you eat? Why are you troubled? Am I not better to you than ten sons?"

⁹ On one occasion, Hannah got up after they ate and drank at Shiloh. The priest Eli was sitting on a chair by the doorpost of the Lord's temple. ¹⁰ Deeply hurt, Hannah prayed to the Lord and wept with many tears. ¹¹ Making a vow, she pleaded, "**Lord of Armies**, if you will take notice of your servant's affliction, remember and not forget me, and give your servant a son, I will give him to the Lord all the days of his life, and his hair will never be cut."

2 SAMUEL 7:22–29

²² This is why you are great, Lord God. There is no one like you, and there is no God besides you, as all we have heard confirms. ²³ And who is like your people Israel? God came to one nation on earth in order to redeem a people for himself, to make a name for himself, and to perform for them great and awesome acts, driving out nations and their gods before your people you redeemed for yourself from Egypt. ²⁴ You established your people Israel to be your own people forever, and you, Lord, have become their God.

²⁵ Now, Lord God, fulfill the promise forever that you have made to your servant and his house. Do as you have promised, ²⁶ so that your name will be exalted forever, when it is said, "The **Lord of Armies** is God over Israel." The house of your servant David will be established before you ²⁷ since you, **Lord of Armies**, God of Israel, have revealed this to your servant when you said, "I will build a house for you." Therefore, your servant has found the courage to pray this prayer to you. ²⁸ Lord God, you are God; your words are true, and you have promised this good thing to your servant. ²⁹ Now, please bless your servant's house so that it will continue before you forever. For you, Lord God, have spoken, and with your blessing your servant's house will be blessed forever.

PSALM 80:4–7

YAHWEH ELOHIM TSEBAOTH

⁴ **Lord God of Armies,**
how long will you be angry
with your people's prayers?
⁵ You fed them the bread of tears
and gave them a full measure
of tears to drink.
⁶ You put us at odds with our neighbors;
our enemies mock us.

ELOHIM TSEBAOTH

⁷ Restore us, **God of Armies**;
make your face shine on us, so that
   we may be saved.

AMOS 5:14–15

¹⁴ Pursue good and not evil
so that you may live,
and the **Lord, the God of Armies**,
will be with you
as you have claimed.
¹⁵ Hate evil and love good;
establish justice in the city gate.
Perhaps the **Lord, the God of Armies**, will be gracious to the remnant of Joseph.

HAGGAI 2:6–9

⁶ For the **Lord of Armies** says this: "Once more, in a little while, I am going to shake the heavens and the earth, the sea and the dry land. ⁷ I will shake all the nations so that the treasures of all the nations will come, and I will fill this house with glory," says the **Lord of Armies**. ⁸ "The silver and gold belong to me"—this is the declaration of the **Lord of Armies**. ⁹ "The final glory of this house will be greater than the first," says the **Lord of Armies**. "I will provide peace in this place"—this is the declaration of the **Lord of Armies**.

MALACHI 1:11–14

¹¹ "My name will be great among the nations, from the rising of the sun to its setting. Incense and pure offerings will be presented in my name in every place because my name will be great among the nations," says the **Lord of Armies.**

¹² "But you are profaning it when you say: 'The Lord's table is defiled, and its product, its food, is contemptible.' ¹³ You also say: 'Look, what a nuisance!' And you scorn it," says the **Lord of Armies**. "You bring stolen, lame, or sick animals. You bring this as an offering! Am I to accept that from your hands?" asks the Lord.

¹⁴ "The deceiver is cursed who has an acceptable male in his flock and makes a vow but sacrifices a defective animal to the Lord. For I am a great King," says the LORD **of Armies**, "and my name will be feared among the nations."

LORD OF ARMIES

What does this name teach me about God?

LUKE 2:13–14

¹³ Suddenly there was a multitude of the heavenly host with the angel, praising God and saying:

¹⁴ Glory to God in the highest heaven,
and peace on earth to people he favors!

1 Sam. 17:45
David

SPIRIT

רוּחַ
RUACH
Hebrew

πνεύμα
PNEUMA
Greek

The non-incarnate, or non-physical, presence of God on earth

KEY OCCURRENCES
NM 11:25; PS 51:10; JN 4:24; 14:17; AC 2:1-4; 10:44-45

The Old Testament contains many references to *ruach*, the Spirit of the Lord, which was the manifestation of God's presence on earth. The New Testament uses *pneuma* for the Holy Spirit, the third person of the Trinity.

In John 4, Jesus tells the woman at the well that God is spirit. He was referring to the time, which has now come, when the Spirit of the Lord would no longer reside in temples built by human hands. Instead, the Holy Spirit dwells inside those who believe in Jesus.

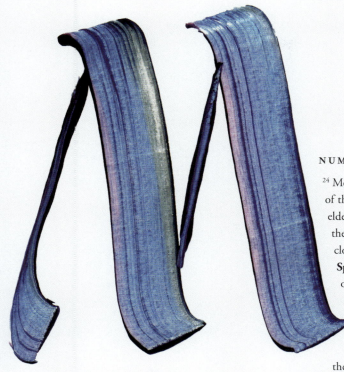

RUACH

NUMBERS 11:24–30

²⁴ Moses went out and told the people the words of the Lord. He brought seventy men from the elders of the people and had them stand around the tent. ²⁵ Then the Lord descended in the cloud and spoke to him. He took some of the **Spirit** that was on Moses and placed the **Spirit** on the seventy elders. As the **Spirit** rested on them, they prophesied, but they never did it again. ²⁶ Two men had remained in the camp, one named Eldad and the other Medad; the **Spirit** rested on them— they were among those listed, but had not gone out to the tent—and they prophesied in the camp. ²⁷ A young man ran and reported to Moses, "Eldad and Medad are prophesying in the camp."

²⁸ Joshua son of Nun, assistant to Moses since his youth, responded, "Moses, my lord, stop them!"

²⁹ But Moses asked him, "Are you jealous on my account? If only all the Lord's people were prophets and the Lord would place his **Spirit** on them!" ³⁰ Then Moses returned to the camp along with the elders of Israel.

PSALM 51:10–13

¹⁰ God, create a clean heart for me
and renew a steadfast spirit within me.
¹¹ Do not banish me from your presence
or take your Holy **Spirit** from me.
¹² Restore the joy of your salvation to me,
and sustain me by giving me a willing spirit.
¹³ Then I will teach the rebellious your ways,
and sinners will return to you.

SHE READS TRUTH

JOHN 4:19–24

¹⁹ "Sir," the woman replied, "I see that you are a prophet. ²⁰ Our fathers worshiped on this mountain, but you Jews say that the place to worship is in Jerusalem."

²¹ Jesus told her, "Believe me, woman, an hour is coming when you will worship the Father neither on this mountain nor in Jerusalem. ²² You Samaritans worship what you do not know. We worship what we do know, because salvation is from the Jews. ²³ But an hour is coming, and is now here, when the true worshipers will worship the Father in **Spirit** and in truth. Yes, the Father wants such people to worship him.

²⁴ God is spirit, and those who worship him must worship in **Spirit** and in truth."

PNEUMA

JOHN 14:15–26

Another Counselor Promised

¹⁵ "If you love me, you will keep my commands. ¹⁶ And I will ask the Father, and he will give you another Counselor to be with you forever. ¹⁷ He is the **Spirit** of truth. The world is unable to receive him because it doesn't see him or know him. But you do know him, because he remains with you and will be in you.

The Father, the Son, and the Holy Spirit

¹⁸ "I will not leave you as orphans; I am coming to you. ¹⁹ In a little while the world will no longer see me, but you will see me. Because I live, you will live too. ²⁰ On that day you will know that I am in my Father, you are in me, and I am in you. ²¹ The one who has my commands and keeps them is the one who loves me. And the one who loves me will be loved by my Father. I also will love him and will reveal myself to him."

²² Judas (not Iscariot) said to him, "Lord, how is it you're going to reveal yourself to us and not to the world?"

²³ Jesus answered, "If anyone loves me, he will keep my word. My Father will love him, and we will come to him and make our home with him. ²⁴ The one who doesn't love me will not keep my words. The word that you hear is not mine but is from the Father who sent me.

²⁵ "I have spoken these things to you while I remain with you. ²⁶ But the Counselor, the Holy **Spirit**, whom the Father will send in my name, will teach you all things and remind you of everything I have told you.

ACTS 2:1–4

Pentecost

¹ When the day of Pentecost had arrived, they were all together in one place. ² Suddenly a sound like that of a violent rushing wind came from heaven, and it filled the whole house where they were staying. ³ They saw tongues like flames of fire that separated and rested on each one of them. ⁴ Then they were all filled with the Holy **Spirit** and began to speak in different tongues, as the **Spirit** enabled them.

ACTS 10:44–48

Gentile Conversion and Baptism

⁴⁴ While Peter was still speaking these words, the Holy **Spirit** came down on all those who heard the message. ⁴⁵ The circumcised believers who had come with Peter were amazed because the gift of the Holy **Spirit** had been poured out even on the Gentiles. ⁴⁶ For they heard them speaking in other tongues and declaring the greatness of God.

Then Peter responded, ⁴⁷ "Can anyone withhold water and prevent these people from being baptized, who have received the Holy **Spirit** just as we have?" ⁴⁸ He commanded them to be baptized in the name of Jesus Christ. Then they asked him to stay for a few days.

SPIRIT

What does this name
teach me about God?

LIVING GOD & GOD MOST HIGH

אֱלֹהִים חַי

ELOHIM CHAY

Hebrew

אֵל עֶלְיוֹן

EL ELYON

Hebrew

God's superiority over all other gods and idols

KEY OCCURRENCES

GN 14:19-20; DT 5:26; 2KG 19:16; PS 84:2; 91:1; JR 10:10; HS 1:10

Elohim Chay, "Living God," and *El Elyon*, "God Most High," are two of the most frequently used names for God in the Old Testament. The name *Elohim* was paired with adjectives that described the God of Israel. These two names, though different, are related. They are used to emphasize the unique nature of God: He is alive and greater than all others.

The very notion of a living God distinguished *Elohim* from idols constructed of wood or iron. The Israelite God was—and is—living and active in and among His people. Similarly, the name "God Most High" elevates the God of Israel over all other gods. These names are reminders that God is active and superior to all other objects of worship.

GENESIS 14:17–20

Melchizedek's Blessing

EL ELYON

¹⁷ After Abram returned from defeating Chedorlaomer and the kings who were with him, the king of Sodom went out to meet him in the Shaveh Valley (that is, the King's Valley). ¹⁸ Melchizedek, king of Salem, brought out bread and wine; he was a priest to **God Most High**. ¹⁹ He blessed him and said:

> Abram is blessed by **God Most High**,
> Creator of heaven and earth,
> ²⁰ and blessed be **God Most High**
> who has handed over your enemies to you.

And Abram gave him a tenth of everything.

2 KINGS 19:14–18

Hezekiah's Prayer

ELOHIM CHAY

¹⁴ Hezekiah took the letter from the messengers' hands, read it, then went up to the Lord's temple, and spread it out before the Lord. ¹⁵ Then Hezekiah prayed before the Lord:

> Lord God of Israel, enthroned between the cherubim, you are God—you alone—of all the kingdoms of the earth. You made the heavens and the earth. ¹⁶ Listen closely, Lord, and hear; open your eyes, Lord, and see. Hear the words that Sennacherib has sent to mock the **living God**. ¹⁷ Lord, it is true that the kings of Assyria have devastated the nations and their lands. ¹⁸ They have thrown their gods into the fire, for they were not gods but made by human hands—wood and stone. So they have destroyed them.

PSALM 91

The Protection of the Most High

¹ The one who lives under the protection of the
   Most High
dwells in the shadow of the Almighty.

² I will say concerning the Lord, who is my refuge
   and my fortress,
my God in whom I trust:
³ He himself will rescue you from the bird trap,
from the destructive plague.
⁴ He will cover you with his feathers;
you will take refuge under his wings.
His faithfulness will be a protective shield.
⁵ You will not fear the terror of the night,
the arrow that flies by day,
⁶ the plague that stalks in darkness,
or the pestilence that ravages at noon.
⁷ Though a thousand fall at your side
and ten thousand at your right hand,
the pestilence will not reach you.
⁸ You will only see it with your eyes
and witness the punishment of the wicked.

⁹ Because you have made the Lord—my refuge,
the **Most High**—your dwelling place,
¹⁰ no harm will come to you;
no plague will come near your tent.
¹¹ For he will give his angels orders concerning you,
to protect you in all your ways.
¹² They will support you with their hands
so that you will not strike your foot against a stone.
¹³ You will tread on the lion and the cobra;
you will trample the young lion and the serpent.

¹⁴ Because he has his heart set on me,
I will deliver him;
I will protect him because he knows my name.
¹⁵ When he calls out to me, I will answer him;
I will be with him in trouble.
I will rescue him and give him honor.
¹⁶ I will satisfy him with a long life
and show him my salvation.

JEREMIAH 10:10–11

¹⁰ But the Lord is the true God;
he is the **living God** and eternal King.
The earth quakes at his wrath,
and the nations cannot endure his rage.

¹¹ You are to say this to them: "The gods that did not make the heavens and the earth will perish from the earth and from under these heavens."

HOSEA 1:10

Yet the number of the Israelites
will be like the sand of the sea,
which cannot be measured or counted.
And in the place where they were told:
You are not my people,
they will be called: Sons of the **living God**.

1 TIMOTHY 4:10

For this reason we labor and strive, because we have put our hope in the living God, who is the Savior of all people, especially of those who believe.

LIVING GOD & GOD MOST HIGH

What do these names teach me about God?

GOD ALMIGHTY

אֵל שַׁדַּי

EL SHADDAY

Hebrew

God's power over all things

KEY OCCURRENCES
GN 17:1; EX 6:3; RU 1:20–21;
PS 91:1; EZK 1:24

El Shadday, or "God Almighty," is a name God uses to describe Himself throughout the Old Testament. He appears to Abraham in Genesis 17 with the greeting, "I am God Almighty." Then God makes a covenant with Abraham, promising to make him the father of a great nation, even though Abraham was old and his wife was barren. God offered His name, God Almighty, as the guarantee of this improbable promise. Bound up in God's covenant promise to Abraham is the Lord's proclamation of His power.

The name God Almighty also appears frequently in the book of Job to emphasize God's power over all things. *El Shadday* is a powerful, impressive name for our God.

GENESIS 17:1–8

Covenant Circumcision

EL SHADDAY

¹ When Abram was ninety-nine years old, the LORD appeared to him, saying, "I am **God Almighty**. Live in my presence and be blameless. ² I will set up my covenant between me and you, and I will multiply you greatly."

³ Then Abram fell facedown and God spoke with him: ⁴ "As for me, here is my covenant with you: You will become the father of many nations. ⁵ Your name will no longer be Abram; your name will be Abraham, for I will make you the father of many nations. ⁶ I will make you extremely fruitful and will make nations and kings come from you. ⁷ I will confirm my covenant that is between me and you and your future offspring throughout their generations. It is a permanent covenant to be your God and the God of your offspring after you. ⁸ And to you and your future offspring I will give the land where you are residing—all the land of Canaan—as a permanent possession, and I will be their God."

EXODUS 6:2–5

God Promises Freedom

² Then God spoke to Moses, telling him, "I am the LORD. ³ I appeared to Abraham, Isaac, and Jacob as **God Almighty**. but I was not known to them by my name the LORD.' ⁴ I also established my covenant with them to give them the land of Canaan, the land they lived in as aliens. ⁵ Furthermore, I have heard the groaning of the Israelites, whom the Egyptians are forcing to work as slaves, and I have remembered my covenant."

2 CORINTHIANS 6:14–18

Separation to God

¹⁴ Don't become partners with those who do not believe. For what partnership is there between righteousness and lawlessness? Or what fellowship does light have with darkness? ¹⁵ What agreement does Christ have with Belial? Or what does a believer have in common with an unbeliever? ¹⁶ And what agreement does the temple of God have with idols? For we are the temple of the living God, as God said:

> I will dwell
> and walk among them,
> and I will be their God,
> and they will be my people.

¹⁷ Therefore, come out from among them
and be separate, says the Lord;
do not touch any unclean thing,
and I will welcome you.
¹⁸ And I will be a Father to you,
and you will be sons and daughters to me,
says the Lord Almighty.

REVELATION 11:16–19

¹⁶ The twenty-four elders, who were seated before God on their thrones, fell facedown and worshiped God, ¹⁷ saying,

> We give you thanks, Lord God, the Almighty,
> who is and who was,
> because you have taken your great power
> and have begun to reign.
> ¹⁸ The nations were angry,
> but your wrath has come.
> The time has come
> for the dead to be judged
> and to give the reward
> to your servants the prophets,
> to the saints, and to those who fear your name,
> both small and great,
> and the time has come to destroy
> those who destroy the earth.

¹⁹ Then the temple of God in heaven was opened, and the ark of his covenant appeared in his temple. There were flashes of lightning, rumblings and peals of thunder, an earthquake, and severe hail.

GOD ALMIGHTY

What does this name teach me about God?

Before this known as El Shaddai - God Almighty

Yahweh

Jehovah → God performing what he has promised - furnishing in his hand, he could do them as he pleased. his own work

It was to Moses that God first showed his power of making alterations in nature or working miracles and prodigies

God is never called Jehovah till the heavens & earth were finished

When the Salvation of Saints is complete in eternal life, then he will be known as Jehovah - Revelation 22:13 -

Jehovah - true, firm & constant to his promises, even to be believed

REFUGE & FORTRESS

מַחְסֶה

MACHSEH

Hebrew

מְצוּדָה

METSUDAH

Hebrew

God's protection from external threats

KEY OCCURRENCES

2SM 22:2; PS 18:2; 62:8; 71:3; 73:28; IS 25:4; JL 3:16

When God's people claim He is their refuge or fortress, they are saying He is a safe place in times of trouble. He will take care of them and protect them. King David uses "refuge" frequently to refer to God—a telling admission from the powerful, mighty king of Israel who led victorious armies into battle. This name of God uses the image of finding safety and rest in a city or fortress to communicate the security God's people have in Him.

DEUTERONOMY 33:26–29

²⁶ There is none like the God of Jeshurun,
who rides the heavens to your aid,
the clouds in his majesty.
²⁷ The God of old is your dwelling place,
and underneath are the everlasting arms.
He drives out the enemy before you
and commands, "Destroy!"
²⁸ So Israel dwells securely;
Jacob lives untroubled
in a land of grain and new wine;
even his skies drip with dew.
²⁹ How happy you are, Israel!
Who is like you,
a people saved by the LORD?
He is the shield that protects you,
the sword you boast in.
Your enemies will cringe before you,
and you will tread on their backs.

2 SAMUEL 22:1–3

David's Song of Thanksgiving

¹ David spoke the words of this song to the LORD on the day the LORD rescued him from the grasp of all his enemies and from the grasp of Saul. ² He said:

> METSUDAH

The LORD is my rock, my **fortress**, and my deliverer,
³ my God, my rock where I seek refuge.
My shield, the horn of my salvation, my stronghold,
   my refuge,
and my Savior, you save me from violence.

PSALM 18:1–3

Praise for Deliverance

For the choir director. Of the servant of the LORD, David, who spoke the words of this song to the LORD on the day the LORD rescued him from the grasp of all his enemies and from the power of Saul. He said:

¹ I love you, LORD, my strength.
² The LORD is my rock,
my **fortress**, and my deliverer,
my God, my rock where I seek refuge,
my shield and the horn of my salvation,
my stronghold.
³ I called to the LORD, who is worthy of praise,
and I was saved from my enemies.

PSALM 71:1–8

God's Help in Old Age

¹ LORD, I seek refuge in you;
let me never be disgraced.
² In your justice, rescue and deliver me;
listen closely to me and save me.

³ Be a rock of refuge for me,
where I can always go.
Give the command to save me,
for you are my rock and **fortress**.

⁴ Deliver me, my God, from the power of the wicked,
from the grasp of the unjust and oppressive.
⁵ For you are my hope, Lord GOD,
my confidence from my youth.
⁶ I have leaned on you from birth;
you took me from my mother's womb.
My praise is always about you.
⁷ I am like a miraculous sign to many,
and you are my strong **refuge**.
⁸ My mouth is full of praise
and honor to you all day long.

MACHSEH

ISAIAH 25:1–5

Salvation and Judgment on That Day

¹ LORD, you are my God;
I will exalt you. I will praise your name,
for you have accomplished wonders,
plans formed long ago, with perfect faithfulness.
² For you have turned the city into a pile of rocks,
a fortified city, into ruins;
the fortress of barbarians is no longer a city;
it will never be rebuilt.

NAMES OF GOD

³ Therefore, a strong people will honor you.
The cities of violent nations will fear you.
⁴ For you have been a stronghold for the poor person,
a stronghold for the needy in his distress,
a **refuge** from storms and a shade from heat.
When the breath of the violent
is like a storm against a wall,
⁵ like heat in a dry land,
you will subdue the uproar of barbarians.
As the shade of a cloud cools the heat of the day,
so he will silence the song of the violent.

REFUGE & FORTRESS

What do these names teach me about God?

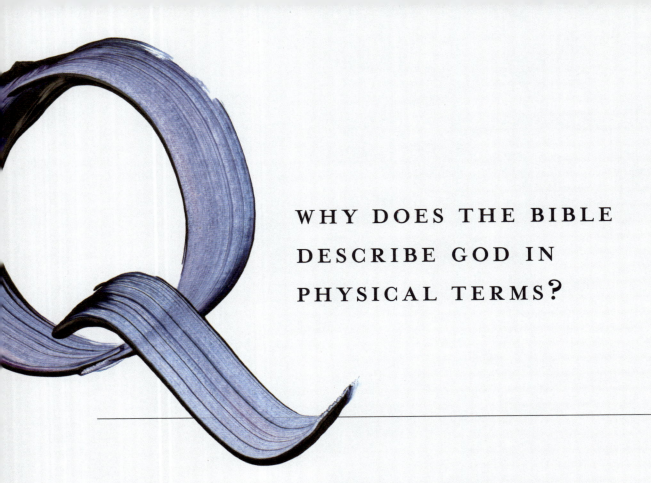

WHY DOES THE BIBLE DESCRIBE GOD IN PHYSICAL TERMS?

Some of God's names in Scripture, like Shepherd, Father, and L ORD of Armies, have their roots in human concepts. The Bible is clear that God is neither visible (Jn 1:18) nor human (1Sm 15:29), yet Scripture often describes God as though He is both.

Scripture compares God to tangible objects.
God is described as a rock (2Sm 22:32), a fortress (Ps 91:2), and a shield (Ps 33:20).

Scripture gives God human titles.
God is described as a king (Ps 24:10), a warrior (Ex 15:3), a judge (Gn 18:25), a bridegroom (Mk 2:19–20), and a friend (Jms 2:23).

Scripture assigns God human attributes.
God is described as having fingers (Dt 9:10), lips (Ps 89:34), shoulders (Dt 33:12), hair (Dn 7:9), and a heart (2Ch 7:16).

Scripture describes God's behavior in human terms.
God is described as someone who builds (Ps 127:1), speaks (Jr 10:1), walks (Dt 23:14), hears (Ps 4:3), and sees (Gn 1:4).

Scripture uses anthropomorphic language—words and phrases that assign human attributes to nonhuman things—to talk about the infinite God in terms finite people can understand.

By using metaphors, analogies, and other concepts we can comprehend, anthropomorphic language helps communicate larger theological truths about the eternal, infinite, invisible God.

13

GRACE DAY

χάρις
CHARIS
Grace

Use this day to pray, rest, and reflect on this week's reading, giving thanks for the grace that is ours in Christ.

Yet the number of the Israelites
will be like the sand of the sea,
which cannot be measured or counted.
And in the place where they were told:
You are not my people,
they will be called: Sons of the living God.

HOSEA 1:10

14

WEEKLY TRUTH

ἀλήθεια

ALÉTHEIA

Truth

Scripture is God-breathed and true. When we memorize it, we carry the gospel with us wherever we go.

This week's verse illustrates that God's revelation of Himself leads us to worship Him.

Lord, you are my God;
I will exalt you. I will praise your name,
for you have accomplished wonders,
plans formed long ago, with perfect faithfulness.

ISAIAH 25:1

Find the corresponding memory card in the back of this book.

JEALOUS GOD

אֵל קַנָּא

EL QANNA

Hebrew

God's right to be the only object of worship

KEY OCCURRENCES
EX 20:5; 34:14; DT 4:24;
JOS 24:19; NAH 1:2

God called Himself a "jealous God" in Exodus 20 when He spoke to Moses at Mount Sinai. This name reminds us that God does not take lightly nor tolerate our wandering hearts. He alone is worthy of our worship and praise, and He will not share it with another.

Scripture presents God as jealous for His deity, His sovereignty, and His glory. Throughout the Old Testament, this name is used to emphasize that He alone is God, and He alone is holy and worthy of our worship.

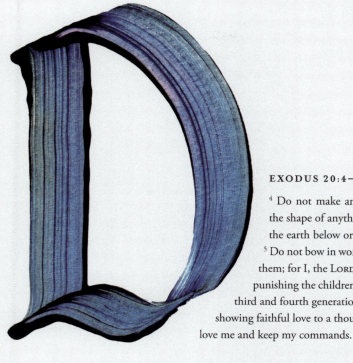

EXODUS 20:4–6

⁴ Do not make an idol for yourself, whether in the shape of anything in the heavens above or on the earth below or in the waters under the earth. ⁵ Do not bow in worship to them, and do not serve them; for I, the Lord your God, am a **jealous God**, punishing the children for the fathers' iniquity, to the third and fourth generations of those who hate me, ⁶ but showing faithful love to a thousand generations of those who love me and keep my commands.

EL QANNA

EXODUS 34:10–16 ESV

The Covenant Renewed

¹⁰ And he said, "Behold, I am making a covenant. Before all your people I will do marvels, such as have not been created in all the earth or in any nation. And all the people among whom you are shall see the work of the Lord, for it is an awesome thing that I will do with you.

¹¹ "Observe what I command you this day. Behold, I will drive out before you the Amorites, the Canaanites, the Hittites, the Perizzites, the Hivites, and the Jebusites. ¹² Take care, lest you make a covenant with the inhabitants of the land to which you go, lest it become a snare in your midst. ¹³ You shall tear down their altars and break their pillars and cut down their Asherim ¹⁴ (for you shall worship no other god, for the Lord, whose name is **Jealous**, is a **jealous God**), ¹⁵ lest you make a covenant with the inhabitants of the land, and when they whore after their gods and sacrifice to their gods and you are invited, you eat of his sacrifice, ¹⁶ and you take of their daughters for your sons, and their daughters whore after their gods and make your sons whore after their gods."

SHE READS TRUTH

DEUTERONOMY 4:23-24

²³ Be careful not to forget the covenant of the Lord your God that he made with you, and make an idol for yourselves in the shape of anything he has forbidden you.

²⁴ For the Lord your God is a consuming fire, a jealous God.

JOSHUA 24:14-20

The Covenant Renewal

¹⁴ "Therefore, fear the Lord and worship him in sincerity and truth. Get rid of the gods your fathers worshiped beyond the Euphrates River and in Egypt, and worship the Lord. ¹⁵ But if it doesn't please you to worship the Lord, choose for yourselves today: Which will you worship—the gods your fathers worshiped beyond the Euphrates River or the gods of the Amorites in whose land you are living? As for me and my family, we will worship the Lord."

¹⁶ The people replied, "We will certainly not abandon the Lord to worship other gods! ¹⁷ For the Lord our God brought us and our fathers out of the land of Egypt, out of the place of slavery, and performed these great signs before our eyes. He also protected us all along the way we went and among all the peoples whose lands we traveled through. ¹⁸ The Lord drove out before us all the peoples, including the Amorites who lived in the land. We too will worship the Lord, because he is our God."

¹⁹ But Joshua told the people, "You will not be able to worship the Lord, because he is a holy God. He is a **jealous God**; he will not forgive your transgressions and sins. ²⁰ If you abandon the Lord and worship foreign gods, he will turn against you, harm you, and completely destroy you, after he has been good to you."

NAHUM 1:1-6

¹ The pronouncement concerning Nineveh. The book of the vision of Nahum the Elkoshite.

God's Vengeance

² The Lord is a **jealous** and avenging **God**;
the Lord takes vengeance
and is fierce in wrath.
The Lord takes vengeance against his foes;
he is furious with his enemies.
³ The Lord is slow to anger but great in power;
the Lord will never leave the guilty unpunished.
His path is in the whirlwind and storm,
and clouds are the dust beneath his feet.
⁴ He rebukes the sea and dries it up,
and he makes all the rivers run dry.
Bashan and Carmel wither;
even the flower of Lebanon withers.
⁵ The mountains quake before him,
and the hills melt;
the earth trembles at his presence—
the world and all who live in it.
⁶ Who can withstand his indignation?
Who can endure his burning anger?
His wrath is poured out like fire;
even rocks are shattered before him.

1 CORINTHIANS 10:14-22

Warning Against Idolatry

¹⁴ So then, my dear friends, flee from idolatry. ¹⁵ I am speaking as to sensible people. Judge for yourselves what I am saying. ¹⁶ The cup of blessing that we bless, is it not a sharing in the blood of Christ? The bread that we break, is it not a sharing in the body of Christ? ¹⁷ Because there is one bread, we who are many are one body, since all of us share the one bread. ¹⁸ Consider the people of Israel. Do not those who eat the sacrifices participate in the altar? ¹⁹ What am I saying then? That food sacrificed to idols is anything, or that an idol is anything? ²⁰ No, but I do say that what they sacrifice, they sacrifice to demons and not to God. I do not want you to be participants with demons! ²¹ You cannot drink the cup of the Lord and the cup of demons. You cannot share in the Lord's table and the table of demons. ²² Or are we provoking the Lord to jealousy? Are we stronger than he?

JEALOUS GOD

What does this name
teach me about God?

WHAT DOES SCRIPTURE SAY ABOUT GOD'S NAME?

In the Bible, names are sacred and often convey identity, significance, character, and relational connection. We see this reflected in the way Scripture talks about God's name.

God's name is holy.

LV 22:32; 1CH 16:35; PS 33:21; LK 1:49

God's name is often synonymous with His reputation.

EX 9:16; JOS 7:8-9; 1SM 12:22; EZK 36:20-23; 39:25; PS 106:7-8

God's people must not use His name in vain.

EX 20:7; LV 19:12; DT 5:11; EZK 39:7; MAL 1:6

God's people are to take on His name sincerely.

DT 28:10; IS 43:6-7; JR 14:9; 15:16; DN 9:19; AC 15:17; RV 14:1

God's people can call on His name.

GN 4:26; 1CH 16:8; PS 91:15; 105:1; ZPH 3:9; AC 2:21

God's people can call Him Father.

IS 54:8; JR 3:19; MT 6:9; LK 11:2; RM 8:15; 1CO 8:6; EPH 1:3

God's name is a refuge for those in trouble.

2SM 22:3; PS 46:1; 91:2; PR 18:10; ZCH 9:12; JR 16:19; NAH 1:7

Christians are to be baptized in the name of the Father, Son, and Holy Spirit.

MT 28:19; AC 22:16; EPH 4:4-6; AC 2:38

SHEPHERD

רֹעִי	רֹעֶה	ποιμήν
RO'I	RO'EH	POIMEN
Hebrew	Hebrew	Greek

God as our provider and caretaker

KEY OCCURRENCES
PS 23:1; EZK 34:12; JN 10:11; HEB 13:20; 1PT 2:25

In Psalm 23, David writes of the Lord as a shepherd: He leads His sheep to calm pasture to eat, He leads them to water to drink, He keeps them on the right path, and He uses His rod and staff to protect them. In John 10, Jesus calls Himself "the Good Shepherd." He outlines His similar responsibilities: He lays down His life to protect His sheep, He gathers His sheep, and He speaks over His sheep. When He takes the name "Shepherd," it doesn't just reveal His role as our protective, sacrificial caretaker; it also reveals our role to remain loyal to and dependent upon Him.

We must allow him to lead us

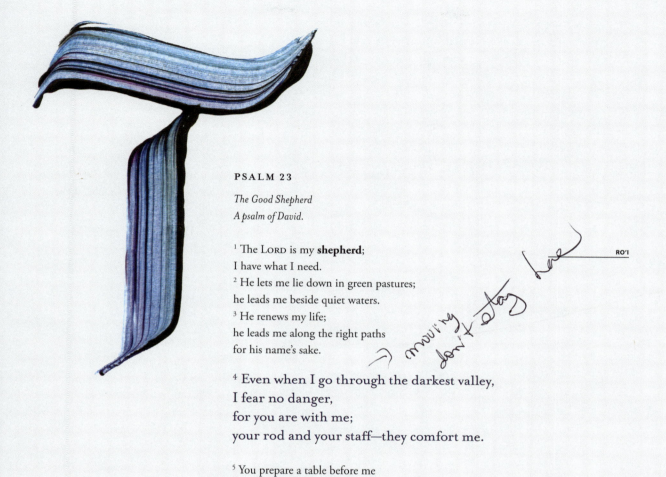

PSALM 23

The Good Shepherd
A psalm of David.

¹ The Lord is my **shepherd**;
I have what I need.
² He lets me lie down in green pastures;
he leads me beside quiet waters.
³ He renews my life;
he leads me along the right paths
for his name's sake.

RO'I

⁴ Even when I go through the darkest valley,
I fear no danger,
for you are with me;
your rod and your staff—they comfort me.

⁵ You prepare a table before me
in the presence of my enemies;
you anoint my head with oil;
my cup overflows.
⁶ Only goodness and faithful love will pursue me
all the days of my life,
and I will dwell in the house of the Lord
as long as I live.

EZEKIEL 34:11–16

¹¹ "For this is what the Lord God says: See, I myself will search for my flock and look for them. ¹² As a **shepherd** looks for his sheep on the day he is among his scattered flock, so I will look for my flock. I will rescue them from all the places where they have

RO'EH

SHE READS TRUTH

been scattered on a day of clouds and total darkness. ¹³ I will bring them out from the peoples, gather them from the countries, and bring them to their own soil. I will shepherd them on the mountains of Israel, in the ravines, and in all the inhabited places of the land. ¹⁴ I will tend them in good pasture, and their grazing place will be on Israel's lofty mountains. There they will lie down in a good grazing place; they will feed in rich pasture on the mountains of Israel. ¹⁵ I will tend my flock and let them lie down. This is the declaration of the Lord God. ¹⁶ I will seek the lost, bring back the strays, bandage the injured, and strengthen the weak, but I will destroy the fat and the strong. I will shepherd them with justice."

JOHN 10:11–18

POIMEN

¹¹ "I am the good **shepherd**. The good **shepherd** lays down his life for the sheep. ¹² The hired hand, since he is not the **shepherd** and doesn't own the sheep, leaves them and runs away when he sees a wolf coming. The wolf then snatches and scatters them. ¹³ This happens because he is a hired hand and doesn't care about the sheep.

¹⁴ "I am the good **shepherd**. I know my own, and my own know me, ¹⁵ just as the Father knows me, and I know the Father. I lay down my life for the sheep. ¹⁶ But I have other sheep that are not from this sheep pen; I must bring them also, and they will listen to my voice. Then there will be one flock, one **shepherd**. ¹⁷ This is why the Father loves me, because I lay down my life so that I may take it up again. ¹⁸ No one takes it from me, but I lay it down on my own. I have the right to lay it down, and I have the right to take it up again. I have received this command from my Father."

HEBREWS 13:20–21

Benediction and Farewell

²⁰ Now may the God of peace, who brought up from the dead our Lord Jesus—the great **Shepherd** of the sheep—through the blood of the everlasting covenant, ²¹ equip you with everything good to do his will, working in us what is pleasing in his sight, through Jesus Christ, to whom be glory forever and ever. Amen.

1 PETER 2:22–25

²² He did not commit sin, and no deceit was found in his mouth; ²³ when he was insulted, he did not insult in return; when he suffered, he did not threaten but entrusted himself to the one who judges justly. ²⁴ He himself bore our sins in his body on the tree; so that, having died to sins, we might live for righteousness. By his wounds you have been healed. ²⁵ For you were like sheep going astray, but you have now returned to the **Shepherd** and Overseer of your souls.

SHEPHERD

What does this name teach me about God?

FATHER

אָב	πατήρ
A B	PATER
Hebrew	*Greek*

The personal, familial, and intimate name for God

KEY OCCURRENCES
DT 32:6; PS 68:5; JR 3:19; MT 6:9; MK 14:36; LK 11:2; RM 8:15; GL 4:6

When Jesus taught His disciples to pray, He told them to address God as "our Father" (Mt 6:9). When He prayed in the Garden of Gethsemane before His arrest, trial, and crucifixion, Jesus cried out, "*Abba*, Father," using personal and relational names for God (Mk 14:36). *Abba* is an Aramaic word, from the Hebrew *Ab*, for "father." *Pater* is the Greek word used for "father."

These are deeply familial names when used to address God. Belief brings us into a close yet respectful relationship with God, the holy Creator of all things. Father is a reverential yet personal name for God.

DEUTERONOMY 32:1-6

Song of Moses

¹ Pay attention, heavens, and I will speak;
listen, earth, to the words from my mouth.
² Let my teaching fall like rain
and my word settle like dew,
like gentle rain on new grass
and showers on tender plants.
³ For I will proclaim the Lord's name.
Declare the greatness of our God!
⁴ The Rock—his work is perfect;
all his ways are just.
A faithful God, without bias,
he is righteous and true.

⁵ His people have acted corruptly toward him;
this is their defect—they are not his children
but a devious and crooked generation.
⁶ Is this how you repay the Lord,
you foolish and senseless people?
Isn't he your **Father** and Creator?
Didn't he make you and sustain you?

AB

PSALM 68:4-6

⁴ Sing to God! Sing praises to his name.
Exalt him who rides on the clouds—
his name is the Lord—and celebrate before him.
⁵ God in his holy dwelling is
a **father** of the fatherless
and a champion of widows.
⁶ God provides homes for those who are deserted.
He leads out the prisoners to prosperity,
but the rebellious live in a scorched land.

JEREMIAH 3:19-22

True Repentance

¹⁹ I thought, "How I long to make you my sons
and give you a desirable land,
the most beautiful inheritance of all the nations."
I thought, "You will call me 'My **Father**'
and never turn away from me."

²⁰ However, as a woman may betray her lover,
so you have betrayed me, house of Israel.
This is the Lord's declaration.

²¹ A sound is heard on the barren heights:
the children of Israel weeping and begging for mercy,
for they have perverted their way;
they have forgotten the Lord their God.

²² Return, you faithless children.
I will heal your unfaithfulness.
"Here we are, coming to you,
for you are the Lord our God."

MARK 14:35-36

³⁵ He went a little farther, fell to the ground, and prayed that if it were possible, the hour might pass from him. ³⁶ And he said, "*Abba*, **Father**! All things are possible for you. Take this cup away from me. Nevertheless, not what I will, but what you will."

PATER

ROMANS 8:14-17

¹⁴ For all those led by God's Spirit are God's sons. ¹⁵ You did not receive a spirit of slavery to fall back into fear. Instead, you received the Spirit of adoption, by whom we cry out, "*Abba*, **Father**!" ¹⁶ The Spirit himself testifies together with our spirit that we are God's children, ¹⁷ and if children, also heirs—heirs of God and coheirs with Christ—if indeed we suffer with him so that we may also be glorified with him.

GALATIANS 4:1-7

¹ Now I say that as long as the heir is a child, he differs in no way from a slave, though he is the owner of everything. ² Instead, he is under guardians and trustees until the time set by his father. ³ In the same way we also, when we were children, were in slavery under the elements of the world. ⁴ When the time came to

completion, God sent his Son, born of a woman, born under the law, ⁵ to redeem those under the law, so that we might receive adoption as sons.

⁶ And because you are sons, God sent the Spirit of his Son into our hearts, crying, "*Abba*, **Father**!"

⁷ So you are no longer a slave but a son, and if a son, then God has made you an heir.

FATHER

What does this name teach me about God?

MESSIAH

מָשִׁיחַ

MASHIACH

Hebrew

Χριστός

CHRISTOS

Greek

God's chosen and anointed one

KEY OCCURRENCES

PS 2:2; MT 16:16; LK 24:26; JN 11:27

The Hebrew word *mashiach*, or "messiah," was used to refer to the promised savior of God's people. The word *mashiach* was translated into the Greek as *christos*, which is translated into English as "Christ." "Messiah" and "Christ" are two titles that describe Jesus as the anointed, or chosen, one of Israel.

The word *mashiach* was used to describe someone who was anointed for a particular calling. In Scripture, people called to serve as prophets, priests, and kings were anointed with oil to ceremonially set them apart for their particular work. Jesus perfectly fulfilled all three of these roles for His people through His life, death, and resurrection. He is the chosen and anointed one who perfectly fulfilled His calling as the savior of God's people.

PSALM 2:1–3

Coronation of the Son

¹ Why do the nations rage
and the peoples plot in vain?
² The kings of the earth take their stand,
and the rulers conspire together
against the Lord and his **Anointed One**　　　──────── MASHIACH
³ "Let's tear off their chains
and throw their ropes off of us."

ISAIAH 61

Messiah's Jubilee

¹ The Spirit of the Lord God is on me,
because the Lord has anointed me
to bring good news to the poor.
He has sent me to heal the brokenhearted,
to proclaim liberty to the captives
and freedom to the prisoners;
² to proclaim the year of the Lord's favor,
and the day of our God's vengeance;
to comfort all who mourn,
³ to provide for those who mourn in Zion;
to give them a crown of beauty instead of ashes,
festive oil instead of mourning,
and splendid clothes instead of despair.
And they will be called righteous trees,
planted by the Lord to glorify him.
⁴ They will rebuild the ancient ruins;
they will restore the former devastations;
they will renew the ruined cities,
the devastations of many generations.

⁵ Strangers will stand and feed your flocks,
and foreigners will be your plowmen and vinedressers.

⁶ But you will be called the Lord's priests;
they will speak of you as ministers of our God;
you will eat the wealth of the nations,
and you will boast in their riches.
⁷ In place of your shame, you will have a double portion;
in place of disgrace, they will rejoice over their share.
So they will possess double in their land,
and eternal joy will be theirs.

⁸ For I the Lord love justice;
I hate robbery and injustice;
I will faithfully reward my people
and make a permanent covenant with them.
⁹ Their descendants will be known among the nations,
and their posterity among the peoples.
All who see them will recognize
that they are a people the Lord has blessed.

¹⁰ I rejoice greatly in the Lord,
I exult in my God;
for he has clothed me with the garments of salvation
and wrapped me in a robe of righteousness,
as a groom wears a turban
and as a bride adorns herself with her jewels.
¹¹ For as the earth produces its growth,
and as a garden enables what is sown to spring up,
so the Lord God will cause righteousness and praise
to spring up before all the nations.

MATTHEW 16:13-20

Peter's Confession of the Messiah

¹³ When Jesus came to the region of Caesarea Philippi, he asked his disciples, "Who do people say that the Son of Man is?"

¹⁴ They replied, "Some say John the Baptist; others, Elijah; still others, Jeremiah or one of the prophets."

¹⁵ "But you," he asked them, "who do you say that I am?"

¹⁶ Simon Peter answered, "You are the **Messiah**, the Son of the living God."

¹⁷ Jesus responded, "Blessed are you, Simon son of Jonah, because flesh and blood did not reveal this to you, but my Father in heaven. ¹⁸ And I also say to you that you are Peter, and on this rock I will build my church, and the gates of Hades will not overpower it. ¹⁹ I will give you the keys of the kingdom of heaven, and whatever you bind on earth will have been bound in heaven, and whatever you loose on earth will have been loosed in heaven." ²⁰ Then he gave the disciples orders to tell no one that he was the **Messiah**.

LUKE 24:18-27

¹⁸ The one named Cleopas answered him, "Are you the only visitor in Jerusalem who doesn't know the things that happened there in these days?"

¹⁹ "What things?" he asked them.

So they said to him, "The things concerning Jesus of Nazareth, who was a prophet powerful in action and speech before God and all the people, ²⁰ and how our chief priests and leaders handed him over to be sentenced to death, and they crucified him. ²¹ But we were hoping that he was the one who was about to redeem Israel. Besides all this, it's the third day since these things happened. ²² Moreover, some women from our group astounded us. They arrived early at the tomb, ²³ and when they didn't find his body, they came and reported that they had seen a vision of angels who said he was alive. ²⁴ Some of those who were with us went to the tomb and found it just as the women had said, but they didn't see him."

²⁵ He said to them, "How foolish and slow you are to believe all that the prophets have spoken! ²⁶ Wasn't it necessary for the **Messiah** to suffer these things and enter into his glory?" ²⁷ Then beginning with Moses and all the Prophets, he interpreted for them the things concerning himself in all the Scriptures.

CHRISTOS

JOHN 10:24–25

²⁴ The Jews surrounded him and asked, "How long are you going to keep us in suspense? If you are the **Messiah**, tell us plainly."

²⁵ "I did tell you and you don't believe," Jesus answered them. "The works that I do in my Father's name testify about me.

JOHN 11:25–27

²⁵ Jesus said to her, "I am the resurrection and the life. The one who believes in me, even if he dies, will live. ²⁶ Everyone who lives and believes in me will never die. Do you believe this?"

²⁷ "Yes, Lord," she told him, "I believe you are the **Messiah**, the Son of God, who comes into the world."

MESSIAH

What does this name teach me about God?

JESUS

יֵשׁוּעַ	Ἰησοῦς
YESHUA	IESOUS
Hebrew	*Greek*

The name of the incarnate Son of God

KEY OCCURRENCES
MT 1:21; AC 4:10; RM 10:9; PHP 2:10–11

The Hebrew name *Yeshua*, or "Jesus," means "Yahweh saves." It is a shortened version of the Hebrew name *Yehoshu'a*, or "Joshua." Jesus, a common name in the first century AD, was the human name the Lord was given on earth. Mary and Joseph obediently gave the child this name because an angel of the Lord visited Joseph in a dream and told him, "you are to name him Jesus, because he will save his people from their sins" (Mt 1:21).

Scripture often combines the name Jesus with the Greek word for messiah, *Christos*, or "Christ." The name "Jesus Christ" joins the two names in order to recognize Jesus as the anointed Savior. The New Testament keeps Jesus's human name and His designation as the Christ linked after the resurrection, emphasizing that He remains fully man and fully God with all authority in heaven and on earth.

JOHN 14:12–14

Praying in Jesus's Name

¹² "Truly I tell you, the one who believes in me will also do the works that I do. And he will do even greater works than these, because I am going to the Father. ¹³ Whatever you ask in my name, I will do it so that the Father may be glorified in the Son. ¹⁴ If you ask me anything in my name, I will do it."

ACTS 4:5–12

Peter and John Face the Jewish Leadership

⁵ The next day, their rulers, elders, and scribes assembled in Jerusalem ⁶ with Annas the high priest, Caiaphas, John, Alexander, and all the members of the high-priestly family. ⁷ After they had Peter and John stand before them, they began to question them: "By what power or in what name have you done this?"

⁸ Then Peter was filled with the Holy Spirit and said to them, "Rulers of the people and elders: ⁹ If we are being examined today about a good deed done to a disabled man, by what means he was healed, ¹⁰ let it be known to all of you and to all the people of Israel, that by the name of **Jesus** Christ of Nazareth, whom you crucified and whom God raised from the dead—by him this man is standing here before you healthy. ¹¹ This **Jesus** is

> the stone rejected by you builders,
> which has become the cornerstone.

¹² There is salvation in no one else, for there is no other name under heaven given to people by which we must be saved."

ROMANS 10:8–13

⁸ On the contrary, what does it say? The message is near you, in your mouth and in your heart. This is the message of faith that we proclaim: ⁹ If you confess with your mouth, "**Jesus** is Lord," and believe in your heart that God raised him from the dead, you will be saved. ¹⁰ One believes with the heart, resulting in righteousness, and one confesses with the mouth, resulting in salvation. ¹¹ For the Scripture says, Everyone who believes on him will not be put to shame, ¹² since there is no distinction between Jew and Greek, because the same Lord of all richly blesses all who call on him. ¹³ For everyone who calls on the name of the Lord will be saved.

PHILIPPIANS 2:5–11

Christ's Humility and Exaltation

⁵ Adopt the same attitude as that of Christ **Jesus**,

> ⁶ who, existing in the form of God,
> did not consider equality with God
> as something to be exploited.
> ⁷ Instead he emptied himself
> by assuming the form of a servant,
> taking on the likeness of humanity.
> And when he had come as a man,
> ⁸ he humbled himself by becoming obedient
> to the point of death—
> even to death on a cross.
> ⁹ For this reason God highly exalted him
> and gave him the name
> that is above every name,
> ¹⁰ so that at the name of **Jesus**
> every knee will bow—
> in heaven and on earth
> and under the earth—
> ¹¹ and every tongue will confess
> that **Jesus** Christ is Lord,
> to the glory of God the Father.

REVELATION 1:4–8

⁴ John: To the seven churches in Asia. Grace and peace to you from the one who is, who was, and who is to come, and from the seven spirits before his throne,

IESOUS

⁵ and from **Jesus** Christ, the faithful witness, the firstborn from the dead and the ruler of the kings of the earth.

To him who loves us and has set us free from our sins by his blood, ⁶ and made us a kingdom, priests to his God and Father—to him be glory and dominion forever and ever. Amen.

⁷ Look, he is coming with the clouds,
and every eye will see him,
even those who pierced him.
And all the tribes of the earth
will mourn over him.
So it is to be. Amen.

⁸ "I am the Alpha and the Omega," says the Lord God, "the one who is, who was, and who is to come, the Almighty."

JESUS

What does this name teach me about God?

GRACE DAY

χάρις
CHARIS
Grace

Use this day to pray, rest, and reflect on this week's reading, giving thanks for the grace that is ours in Christ.

For I will proclaim the LORD's name.
Declare the greatness of our God!
The Rock—his work is perfect;
all his ways are just.
A faithful God, without bias,
he is righteous and true.

DEUTERONOMY 32:3–4

WEEKLY TRUTH

ἀλήθεια

ALĒTHEIA

Truth

Scripture is God-breathed and true. When we memorize it, we carry the gospel with us wherever we go.

This week we will memorize a verse about the strength and power of Jesus's name.

"Whatever you ask in my name,
I will do it so that the Father may
be glorified in the Son."

JOHN 14:13

Find the corresponding memory card in the back of this book.

DOWNLOAD THE APP

STOP BY
shereadstruth.com

SHOP
shopshereadstruth.com

SEND A NOTE
hello@shereadstruth.com

CONNECT
#SheReadsTruth

BIBLIOGRAPHY

Arnold, Clinton E. *How We Got the Bible*. Grand Rapids: Zondervan, 2008.

Berry, John D., ed. *Lexham Bible Dictionary*. Bellingham, WA: Lexham, 2016.

Brown, Francis, S.R. Driver, and Charles A. Briggs. *The Brown-Driver-Briggs Hebrew and English Lexicon*. Peabody, MA: Hendrickson Publishers, 1996.

Comer, John Mark. *God Has a Name*. Grand Rapids: Zondervan, 2017.

Holladay, William L. *A Concise Hebrew and Aramaic Lexicon of the Old Testament*. Grand Rapids: Eerdmans, 1972.

Kittel, Gerhard, Geoffrey W. Bromiley, and Gerhard Friedrich, *Theological Dictionary of the New Testament*. Grand Rapids: Eerdmans, 1976.

Louw, Johannes P., and Eugene Albert Nida, *Greek-English Lexicon of the New Testament: Based on Semantic Domains*. New York: United Bible Societies, 1996.

Myers, Allen C. *The Eerdmans Bible Dictionary*. Grand Rapids: Eerdmans, 2000.

Spangler, Ann, and Lavonne Neff, eds. *The Names of God Bible*. Ada, MI: Revell, 2011.

Spurgeon, C. H. "A Jealous God," March 29, 1863. Metropolitan Tabernacle.

Thomas, Robert L. *New American Standard Hebrew-Aramaic and Greek Dictionaries: Updated Edition*. Anaheim, CA: Foundation Publications, Inc., 1998.

SHE READS TRUTH *is a worldwide community of women who read God's Word together every day.*

Founded in 2012, She Reads Truth invites women of all ages to engage with Scripture through daily reading plans, online conversation led by a vibrant community of contributors, and offline resources created at the intersection of beauty, goodness, and Truth.

FOR THE RECORD

WHERE DID I STUDY?

- ○ HOME
- ○ OFFICE
- ○ COFFEE SHOP
- ○ CHURCH
- ○ A FRIEND'S HOUSE
- ○ OTHER

WHAT WAS I LISTENING TO?

ARTIST:

SONG:

PLAYLIST:

WHEN DID I STUDY?

MORNING

AFTERNOON

NIGHT

My closing prayer:

WHAT WAS HAPPENING IN MY LIFE?

WHAT WAS HAPPENING IN THE WORLD?

| MONTH | DAY | YEAR |

END DATE